Contents

Anna Jackson
Foreword — vii

Carolyn DeCarlo
Winter Swimmers

Spy Valley	3
Tetrachromacy	4
Spirit Animals	6
House	7
Winter Swimmers	8
Redwing	10
Fields of Glass	12
Bigfaced Moons	14
The Car and the Man Inside	16
Winter Swimmers	17
Watch Your Mouth	18
Equilibrium of a Rigid Body	19
The Year I Let My Heart Go Asunder	21
Winter Swimmers	22
Castle Point	23
Roller Coaster Hands	24
Anne Brontë	25
Cosmic Rays	26
Winter Swimmers	27
Hiding	29
Hostage	31
Earthquake Preparedness	34
Winter Swimmers	35

Sophie van Waardenberg
does a potato have a heart?

we are working on standing still	39
unhatched egg/two girls at easter	40
rocky shore	41
red brick, stamford street	42
I only took one photo of switzerland	43
all the friendship bracelet makers	
have retreated	44
to keep all the bees out	45
apricot	46
schön	47
january at the bloemenmarkt	48
complaint	49
do not blame me for loving the	
2003 film love, actually	50
if you cannot draw good pictures	52
it is only the morning	53
this is a coping mechanism	54
I don't remember inviting you	55
unfortunately pam beesly I fell in love	
with you briefly	56
notes on the girls with the red cardigans	57
does a potato have a heart?	58
agape	59
grace wakes late	60

Rebecca Hawkes
Softcore coldsores

Primal scream practice	65
Gremlin in sundress	66
Dairy queen	67
The flexitarian	69
Would I recognise the garden if I saw it	70
The cave draws you in like a breath	72
Cold speculum	73
Add penetrant to preferred broadleaf herbicide	
& devastate the wildflowers	75
The land without teeth	78
Tropical snow	81
Barbecue mirage	82
If I could breed your cultivar I'd have you in my garden	83
Technicolour dreamcake	85
Meanwhile	86
Grooming	88
Overladen trellis	90
Death by nectar	91
Shield your eyes for the bright of it	92
Biologist abandoned	94
Any machine can be a smoke machine	
if you use it wrong enough	96
Crush	98

Notes	103

Foreword

AUP New Poets 5 presents three younger poets, each of whose work stands out for its fierce intelligence, formal command and dazzling vivacity. All three poets are represented by a substantial selection of their work, to give a sense of each poet's distinctive voice while demonstrating something of their range. In this anthology are poems about transformation, beauty and hunger, childhood and coming of age, limpets, mangroves, avocados, the sickly liquid from a smashed and dribbly apple, a stale pie, an eviscerated bird, trilobites, giants, kākā, romance and desire.

Carolyn DeCarlo, originally from the US, is well known in Wellington where she has run the popular literary reading series *Food Court,* produced zines and chapbooks, and read at LitCrawls and other poetry events. I was first charmed and transfixed by Caro's poetry several years ago when I heard her reading co-authored poems in duet with Jackson Nieuwland, and have continued to be dazzled by her work ever since. The poetry she presents in *AUP New Poets 5* is centred around Aro Valley, an Aro Valley transfigured by the imaginative leaps, scientific knowledge, keen observation and sometimes odd habits with which she inhabits it. If in 'Spy Valley' the kākā is an 'eruption' of noise and movement into the poet's reverie, in the poem 'Tetrachromacy' that follows it she considers the bird's point of view, and the 'hyperreal glory' of a life seen with four instead of three colour cones. Cats appear with 'person-eyes in front of mine, / set in their frame of orange fur' and it seems perfectly natural to consider that 'if you were an insect you might be a crane fly'. Being human, in fact, often seems stranger than being a more ordinary animal or plant: in 'Winter Swimmers' she muses that 'It is a privilege to lift / our toes off the sandy bed / and not grow roots, / buoyed up by saline, / oxygenated sacs / hanging at our ribcages'. A surrealism can emerge from the intensity of her imaginative empathy, from a piece of word play or word slippage

– as when the wind blows 'rain in ghosts across the bush' – and from the repeated shifts in perspective and scale. In 'The Year I Let My Heart Go Asunder' the poet imagines herself a giant 'huge as the hills ... squatting with my bottom on Khandallah, / my feet in the harbour and the water barely splashing my ankles'. She knows herself to be wondrous, but she is no spectacle, pushing away 'the men in their cars and their ships and their helicopters / slowly circling' without violence or force, just by bending reality with her mind. Wondrous is a word I would use, too, for DeCarlo's *AUP New Poets 5* selection. This is poetry that is powerful and yet gentle at the same time, tender and enormous in its attention to the drama and detail of everyday life.

Sophie van Waardenberg is currently working at the Open Book in Ponsonby, having recently completed her BA at Auckland University, but will be moving to the US shortly to undertake an MFA in poetry at Syracuse University, New York State. I have found the poetry she has published in literary journals such as *Starling* and *Mimicry*, and which has appeared on *The Spinoff* and *Best New Zealand Poems*, unforgettable for the freshness and lyricism with which it evokes childhood, friendship and love. There is a wonderful airiness to these poems. Even the smallest, most compact poems, like 'rocky shore' and 'apricot', open up and move in ways a limpet doesn't ('imagine the charge of the light brigade / but with limpets'). The longer poems, meanwhile, have a spaciousness and lightness to them, with poems like 'january at the bloemenmarkt' spreading phrases out across the page with the liberal use of the tab key suggesting the sunlight and air, the distractions and longing, that fill the space of the poem. Unlike the limpet, the poet is not going to spend her life 'with [her] tongue stuck to a rock', and several poems are concerned with the wonder and vulnerability of travel, the loneliness of not knowing what you are missing, 'home' or 'her or her', or missing very specifically one loved and desired person in particular, getting to know strangers by the different ways they eat avocados, sharing photos 'to prove I am succeeding', to Velcro yourself across continents to those you miss most. One poem describes the poet 'full of maybe' but these poems are full of certainties, too, especially certainties of affection, and full of 'foliage … all growing, all well'.

Rebecca Hawkes grew up on a high-country sheep and beef farm near Methven, moving to Wellington in 2013 to graduate in media studies and completing an MA in creative non-fiction at Victoria University. The lush visual detail of her poetry can be seen in her paintings, too, which she describes as 'sugar-coated surrealities' influenced by the work of the Pre-Raphaelites and botanical art, and which are as gorgeous and disturbing as her poetry. Language begins, she suggests in the poem that opens her selection, as erosion and anchor, as hunger and control, a way to make a place for the self 'that is not inside of anyone else', a way 'to hold something / and have it not fall apart'. These are poems obsessed with processes of control and decay, finding each as disturbing and as desirable as the other. The precision of the imagery ravishes even when she is describing 'fingers / dyed greenish by weeks of cowpat splashback' or a headache that 'glitters in my lobes' and has to be watered down 'with a dose of sparkling sav'. There is a tremendous hunger expressed for all kinds of nourishment, an openness to the intensity of the world: waking early and walking hungry she finds 'the light so cold & loud it clangs like a cutlery drawer in anger'; in response 'my pores whorl open into spiracles that gasp for extra air'. Alive to the prettiness of the 'deep rooted & pernicious' lupins that divide opinion amongst farmers she knows, she is wary of a 'sentimental glut / unearned emotions   a / too-easy picturesque' but cannot help relishing 'their bright disaster of seeds'. The lush resources of language are relished too, with gorgeous sentence after gorgeous sentence cascading through this selection: when you find yourself not in love but in a cave, you encounter 'a reassurance of creamy calcite catacombing you amid its fossils'. Entering caves and lingering in carparks, moving between the meat aisle of a supermarket and a doctor's surgery, between mangrove swamp and discotheque, these poems have a tremendous imaginative reach, conjuring up a Circe who claims to be anti-vaccination (because she is against the continuation of the human race), a werewolf embarrassed at school, unpruned vines that grasp like Icarus at the closest star, and a disturbingly hostile and erotic relationship with a golem. In the poem 'Would I recognise the garden if I saw it' she writes, 'sweetness pierces the tongue like a staplegun' – which is rather the effect these poems have on me.

AUP New Poets was launched in 1999 under the editorship of Elizabeth Caffin, and my own poetry was included in the first anthology of the series along with poetry by Raewyn Alexander and Sarah Quigley. Further *New Poets* anthologies were published in 2002 and 2008, with the most recent anthology, *AUP New Poets 4*, edited by Anna Hodge, launching the careers of Harry Jones, Erin Scudder and Chris Tse in 2011. With so much exciting and original poetry by younger poets circulating on the internet, read in crowded bookshops or packed-out bars, and appearing in lively print and online literary journals like *Starling, Sweet Mammalian, Blackmail Press, Ika* and *Mimicry*, it seems like a good time to relaunch this series of anthologies, and exciting to be able to do so with poetry as gorgeous and extraordinary as these selections by Carolyn DeCarlo, Sophie van Waardenberg and Rebecca Hawkes.

Anna Jackson

Carolyn DeCarlo

Winter Swimmers

Spy Valley

Mauve colours the sky over Spy Valley,
churning a hazy film that deadens bones,
holds things still and deep in its grip.
Nothing moves, all is quiet,
captive in the lush grey wash
tingeing all the houses and fences
and faces upturned to the sky.
A dry wind sounds up from the core
of the valley, moving stealthily,
rasping up its walls in waves.
You could catch the movement
then, if you were looking at the trees –
but you're not. You're deep in the murky
light blanketing the bush, the ferns, and
down, down into the city with all its cars
and the harbour with all its boats,
all their starry lights switching on,
moving forward, steady, steady in the dusk.
It erupts then, the kākā brash and red,
swooning overhead in the evening sky,
picking up speed, claiming this,
this is mine. Their calls cleave the
valley like lightning, crackling in the air,
striking the dirt beneath your toes,
and when the drops of rain hit your face
thick as bread you're unafraid,
you open wide, you spread your arms
and soak your skin in anguine heat,
its spongy hug lulling you into sleep.

Tetrachromacy

The needle presses into the groove
as wind pushes across the valley,
carrying the rain in ghosts across the bush,
horizontal, transparent sheaths
sending birds back to their nests,
back to their childhoods.

The cat bodies are pink and black
as pigs below the fur,
their claws tearing off
the meaty bits in fear,
padded fingers
fumbling at barb, at rachis,
at vane – catching,
when one is very lucky,
at hollow shaft, at quill,
and plucking a single iridescent feather
from the bird, a shock of red
adorning whiskered mouth
to be deposited at the foot of the door
as a talisman,
an omen – properties unclear.

The kākā wakes
to the hyperreal glory of life,
its four-dimensional colour space
undampened by the underbrush,
enhanced in the dim basin,
soaring in primary light.

Count the pigments in our cone cells
and add one for luck, for flight,
for endless, outstretched nights
from tip to tip,
for everything we lack,

fitting narrowed bloodstreams
into the colour channels overhead,
four valves to pump from
just the same as us –
the lungs,
a thrumming in the throat,
a clutch of sacs held close to the tail.

Ultraviolet washes over the valley,
picks apart the light,
extends vision across the range.
The kākā swans down low and,
looping its own vocal fry,
plucks the feather from its maw,
glittering whole against muted tones,
baring its throat to the night.

Spirit Animals

Outside of time, the spirits slink.
A thread is a thread is a thread
I pull it and it's still a thread.

Dirt and nails and bones
are the only things keeping me together.
Dirt and nails and bones
do not apply here.

I can tell a lot about a person
by the way their carpet smells.

I climbed a hill for seventy days.
On the seventy-first day I reached the top.
On the seventy-second day it all got easier.
On the seventy-third day I was a dead thing.

Seventy-four ways of looking at my own nose.

I timed myself jumping off the Empire State Building
forty-six times in a row.
By the forty-fifth time I could do it in under 12 seconds flat.
The trick didn't have anything to do with aerodynamics.
It didn't matter whether I kept my legs together or not
all I had to do was swallow eight pennies on the way up.

Someone is swallowing a catfish in a forest in Germany right now.
Someone is walking on top of the Salt Lake.
Someone is having a seance in their backyard in Rotorua,
making sulphuric potions for all their best mates.

Today I bought an urn that will turn me into a tree.
Tomorrow I will buy a cat that can turn me into a cat
that can turn cats into dead things.
On Wednesday I will turn a cat into a tree.

House

I tie a thread around my ankles
and lower my body down
beneath the deck
to watch the cats with human faces
clean themselves in the half-light
of their homes.

A zeppelin disguised as a kererū
propels itself magnificently
through the troposphere overhead
and my person-eyes are transfixed
by the person-eyes in front of mine,
set in their frame of orange fur.

How far back does the person go,
I wonder –
as in, are they person-brains or cat-brains
living inside?

The cats' homes are so clean,
pitched roofs and whitewashed boards
fitted snug to the land,
the gentle roll of the hill.
It is hard to hold onto them,
hard to keep sight of their scale
as we tap dance on the lino
above their heads.

Winter Swimmers

Shivers pass through their fingers,
the winter swimmers
anchored below.

They gaze up from their places
in the gelled silence,
bodies swaying –
unweighted, suspended.

We drift on the surface,
obeying the currents,
all snorkels and goggles
fogged up in excitement.

It is a privilege to lift
our toes off the sandy bed
and not grow roots,
buoyed up by saline,
oxygenated sacs
hanging at our ribcages.

They have been before us,
the winter swimmers,
and left long ago
below, in quiet places.

Our feet brush against their hair
as we kick on,
bending back to flip
over and over, never tiring,
eyes open to the light
playing fractals on the surface.

We have gone far,
chasing brightly coloured scales,
the shore a thin strip
tearing open the horizon.

We cannot guess the depth,
diving down to cup the water,
pushing it behind,
catching –
just for a second –
a white glint beyond the deep.

Redwing

Tiny footsteps crash
upon the ceiling.
You hit them with your fist,
eyes charged through
with green,
but too hard –
and all the trees come down
with a bang.

I don't like when I can smell
the others' meat through the walls.
Lying on the carpet with your nose
pressed to the fibres
you say it's only lava
coming in through the cracks,
but I can tell the difference
when it's mixing with ours.

Outside, the fronds are unfurling.
They stayed tight and brown
all through the cold.
We thought they might stay
like that forever.
They uncoiled themselves
first by their spines, then laterally,
one after the next
so fast we could barely keep up.

A kākā came in off the wind
when you opened the door,
piercing your back.
You itched and itched,
pushing your back against
the groove in the headboard.
This morning, buds appeared
under your skin,
small white beads as hard as nuts.

I am afraid to touch them,
afraid I'll crush them up
like coriander
in the mortar and pestle
or snail's shells
under my shoes in the night.

Fields of Glass

I stand on the glass hill
and watch a man litter,
the pamphlet floating
from his pocket onto the street.
He is careless
in a way you think you are not.

When is it red?
When is it red on your face?
The woman kicks the pamphlet
with her big shoe.

Some days, the building looks
uncomfortable. Some days
the building is sad and green.
There is a glass box at the top
of the building for us to visit in.
The box is painted black.
If you stand in the middle,
you can see the whole city.

Once I saw a man in there.
He said it wasn't fun.
He told me to go to the mountain
but I hate climbing.
Climbing makes my knees go funny.

Another time, we danced
on the floor. Do you remember that?
Our socks bunched up
around our ankles
then our ankles around our knees
and so on.

I am eating tomatoes and crying.
If you sit beside me
I will let you carry the juice.
I am carrying the rain.

Bigfaced Moons

Big Man squeezes the cars down into pancakes,
flattens them into the bitumen
until their wheels are the tallest things.

Sleek disks slide down the streets,
dropping tiny people off at the corners.

The moon's light reflects off their backs,
bigfaced moons bouncing back and forth
between earth and the outersphere.

Where does all the light come from, you ask,
and Big Man crushes another car.
That's easy, he says, light comes from Big Man.

That's not quite right,
one of the tiny people says
from down low on the concrete
at the corner of Tory and Vivian.

Where do all the tiny people come from, you ask,
but Big Man is on Taranaki by now and he can't hear,
big legs shaking the lightbulbs loose all the way up the hill.

A tiny person is holding onto your shoelace,
his left ear sliding up your ankle bone with every step
like a tiny caress.

Broken glass litters the footpath ahead of you
and you're happy the bigfaced moon is out tonight.
Big Man rounds the corner and disappears.
When is the next astronaut going up, you ask,
at least tell me that.

A tan moth peeks out from the curtain
when you pass the old dog's house.
You listen for Big Man's response but all you hear
is the laughter from seven tiny people gathered at the next corner.

The Car and the Man Inside

They were buried there,
the car and the man inside,
swept over with a blanket
of copper leaves
under the pavement
in front of the house
at the end of the street.

Everyone knew about them,
the car and the man inside,
and even when we played
catch-the-toad
with the neighbours' cars
we stayed away.

The closest we ever got
was the time Eddie
pushed Billy onto
the crack in the asphalt
where they came out from under
the pavement at night,
the car and the man inside.

The red leaked out of Billy's hair
into the crack and we all ran away
except Sarah Beth, who stopped to trace
his outline with sidewalk chalk.

Billy had a seam of stitches
from neck to crown
when he came home.
His shoulders are still marked
on the pavement in yellow chalk.

Winter Swimmers

Binoculars held aloft,
your twinned lenses
sweep the valley's bouquet,
heads of broccoli
displayed as in a supermarket.

Watch the birds
diving down into their ears,
the ascent just as abrupt –
startled by fleshy bodies
laid out on the boughs
weaving lies into the trees.

They wait for darkness to cover them
in sheets of water,
the beaded blanket descending
on white clouds, settling down,
tucked in tight for the night.

Blackness is sudden,
a clap, and the bodies
invisible in the rain.
Just a creak of joints
betrays them,
a gasp of thread
breaking in the wind.

Watch Your Mouth

I am creating the scaffolding for my own skin,
the fatty tissues that build layer after layer,
sweat glands coiled tight,
nerves kinked like a garden hose.
You grow inside of me and I feel myself rising up
like dough, skin expanding exponentially.

I am stuck in the daily concerns of myself,
the spread of my thighs, clothes splitting at the seams.
Swathe my body in yards of silks and French cottons.
Show me how to contour the new contours of myself.

I rub lotion all over my stomach and realise
I am rubbing lotion all over you.
When will we stop expanding?
I turn circles in the mirror,
checking to see where we end,
checking the calendar to see when it will all end.

I feel you snaking across the breadth of my hips,
turning circles inside my breasts and ass.
I am sceptical that you ever spent a day inside my uterus.

I am a room full of objects waiting to be compressed.
Lift up my body and place the swell of it upon a million feathers.
Unravel the folds of me across the Pacific Ocean.
I am massive. I want to be weightless.

Equilibrium of a Rigid Body

Think about the things you like,
like an old brooch or a handful of gemstones,
fresh cut grass between your fingers or
the smell of a flower you picked
in the gardens in Hamilton last summer,
the one you can never remember the name for.

You'll need them all next winter
when your legs grow numb
and you sit at work thinking about degeneration
until you feel like you're rising up out of your body.

Get a glass of water,
close your eyes, and breathe deeply.
Take the time to do this even when others are watching.
Remember the times this has happened to you before,
walking across campus two years prior
or for the first time, at the end of a run,
back when you were a student yourself.

This will help you keep perspective.
You are not dying.
You are not going to be captured
and put in a wheelchair
like when you were at the airport
and the woman in the United Airlines uniform
told you it was the only way you'd make it to your flight.

Don't have flashbacks to this
or to when you sat cross-legged on Venice Beach for so long
that when you tried to stand your legs had gone numb
from the waist down and you had to crawl on your hands and knees
in the sand thinking, this is what it feels like to be paralysed.

These are normal things,
they happen to everyone,
so don't worry.
Everyone around you is just as uncomfortable as you are.

Breathe and keep breathing.
Drink water and keep drinking.
Don't go to work when you're in pain.
Working in an office isn't good for your body
and it is important to maintain your health
when your soul feels so light
it might float away one morning
without you even realising it.

The Year I Let My Heart Go Asunder

Scraping into the basin with both hands
I let the waves lap against them,
pushing my giant hands to and fro.
The waves are gentle and they make my hands bob
like moths do when they're not being harassed by lights.

I am crouched down on the bank of Wellington Harbour
and I am huge as the hills.
I am squatting with my bottom on Khandallah,
my feet in the harbour and the water barely splashing my ankles.

When I stand, I am wondrous.

Get back! I want to cry out
at the men in their cars and their ships and their helicopters
slowly circling.
Get away, don't look.

I push them, but not with my hands
just with my mind,
not hurting them but just bending –
bending them with my mind until they go.

Winter Swimmers

Wind carves through the trees
like waves,
the sound indiscernible
from the ocean.
We can see the harbour
if we stand outside,
our bare feet on the rough boards
creaking like a ship.
In this house
we will never be more than
8 km from the sea.

New green
covers the tops of the ferns,
spreading the valley
with startling pigment,
the old brown lengths hovering
then sinking below.
It is a comfort
to see them go,
a comfort to watch
the new patches
ease in, grow darker,
shouldering down
to take their place.

Pull back on the net of time
and return to the Age of Fish,
their first bones scattered
amongst the trilobites
beneath the seas
and spores and spores
swelling up into trees,
drinking in their waters
high above the waves.

Castle Point

Sperm whales
are distinguishable
by the crashing sound
they make
on the surface.

We sit on the cliff
eating hot cross buns
and waiting for
the whales to breathe.

What will we do with ourselves
this afternoon,
and the day after that,
and the next thirty years?

I will wake up next to you
and keep waking up
next to you.

Roller Coaster Hands

Your hands are a roller coaster on my legs.
Tiny children ride your hands and say whee!
They like the part of the ride where your hand
races down my thigh to my knee the best,
although the part where you spin your hand
in a circle on my calf is pretty good too.

I went to Coney Island and watched a ride break down.
People in sticky uniforms helped kids climb
from one car to the next across the ride.
Each car was shaped like a log.
Some kids straddled the log and scooted
because they were too afraid to walk,
even with the attendant's hand.

We rode the tilt-a-whirl, laughing in line
because all the other riders were so small.
We sat with our knees against the bar,
holding it up with our hands, too big to lock it in place.
We took photos, pretending to be the kids with wide grins.
Then the ride started, and on the first spin
our stomachs dropped and we became so small.

Anne Brontë

If I were an insect, I might be a lightning bug
but you would call me a firefly.
If you were an insect you might be a crane fly.
I don't know what I would call you.
You're not my kind of daddy long-legs.

If you were a crane fly your legs would be deciduous,
meaning: tending to fall off, particularly at maturity.
You might still have them
but you'd be getting close to losing them.
We're getting close to losing our immaturity.

I bought a book about leaves for my father
but I want to keep it for myself.
We live in the bush now and it takes too long to get anywhere
so I might just stay up here this year,
carrying his book with me along the trails behind our house.
I'll buy a pair of binoculars and spy on all the birds
and think of them as my friends because the neighbour's cats won't
    talk to me,
they just stare at me through the windows until I move
and then hunch down under the porch.

If we were Brontë sisters,
I would be Anne and you would be Emily.

Cosmic Rays

Our bones are radioactive.
If we were made of plants,
we might be more radioactive
but all of our radioactivity
is second-hand,
a product of ingesting plants
for days and days and days.

Our bones show our age like trees:
cut us open and you will see our rings,
cut us open and you will see our plants.
We are living free of carbon dioxide.
We are practising radioactive decay.
In 50,000 years we will be ageless.

As a tree grows, only its outermost ring
inhales carbon.
As a tree grows, only its outermost ring
is made of bone.
As a tree grows, only its outermost ring
knows bark knows skin knows air.
Trees grow from the inside,
some rings will never reach the surface.

Winter Swimmers

We are not
swimming pools,

our faces
never submerged in water
long enough to breathe,

never dipped
below the surface,
eyes absorbing the
chlorine and urea
flushing milky pink.

We do not
share the sunblock,

our fingers
wet and greasy
against each other's backs,

never slipping
out of hands
and towels and lycra
to perform our skin
against the density
of $1,000.00$ kg/m^3.

We do not
scrape the balls of our feet
against the concrete

playing spider
in the corners,
nor do our toes
gather grains of sand

to be sucked out later
in the bathroom
by hungry lifeguards.

We are in pieces,
not limited by bodies
of water and skin,

we turn ourselves
inside, we float up
like plastic bags
on the sea,
rising to form clouds.

Hiding

Oh, look! The sky
is all turning orange
and the clouds are dipped
in pink. It's so hot
in here and I need to pee
and anyway I can go
upstairs and make a cup
of tea and then I can
stand outside and watch
them. I forgot
about the fish since
the last time I saw them.
What if they really needed
a human to help them?
They would be dead
by now. Someone
might take care of them,
like whoever washes the
tea towels, but I left
some water in the kettle.
It's nice to feel the cold
air on my face. My
cheeks have been getting
so hot lately and I don't
know why. The sky
is all nice and red
now with those
dark grey clouds in
front. Actually, it's
kind of frightening
the way they're doing that,
the red is too deep,
and those black bits
wisping down,
kind of demonic when

you think about it. It
would be funny if
someone came along
the path now and found me
here, staring at the clouds.
I could tell them about
how demonic they look,
though. Oh, look! Here
comes Eamonn with his
backpack on, I can tell
him. I wonder if he's
been at school all day.
I hope I don't scare him
standing in the middle of
the bushes on the path
here, but anyway that might be
kind of funny. What should
I say? Oh, he's walking up
the back steps now.
Should I shout?
Never mind, he's gone.
It's easy to hide yourself
here, easy to stay
hidden. I didn't know I could
be so hidden.

Hostage

I want to live in beauty,
she thinks,
the ball of her foot
pressed
against the pedal,

her eyes
on the truck
ahead of her,

her eyes
ticking across
the candied apple finish,
so slick she can taste it,
the stamped metal
of the licence plate
painted in white and blue,
'wild, wonderful',
the large metal cylinders –
what are they, pipes? –
stacked in a pyramid
on the bed of the truck,

being carried.
They seem patient.

She focuses on the cylinders,
grouped together
and tied with a length of plastic
like a bouquet of flowers
or a group of girls
taken hostage,
imagines them
talking to each other,
hugging, kissing, fighting.

She imagines
one cylinder
breaking away,
one cylinder
and the whole pyramid
gives.
She imagines them
sliding
from the back of the truck
like seals, diving
into her windshield
like they do in movies.

She imagines
one or more cylinders
pushing into her mouth,
pushing her teeth back
into her skull.
She thinks about it
until she can taste the metal,
until the taste of the metal
is under her face
and her nails
and her tongue,

until she can picture
her car flipping off the road,
a man in a windbreaker
pulling her from the car
while her mouth bleeds
and mid-2000s dream pop
plays in the background.

She thinks about
switching lanes,
speeding up,
passing the red truck
and its hollow cylinders.

She thinks about
how much better she would be
at giving oral sex
with her teeth pressed up
into her skull.

Earthquake Preparedness

Little fibres break inside my calves.
That is how I know I'm alive
when I'm climbing up the hill
making all the wooshing noises
in my chest and mouth.

A couple in jogging shorts
turns and stares.
They can hear the popping in my calves
and they know that I'm alive.

Denim circle skirts are
tomorrow's jogging shorts
like yesterday's sequinned tube top was
today's hi-vis vest.

I stole it
from the earthquake preparedness closet at work,
and this helmet and this bicycle.
The closet is significantly less prepared now.

Someone at work has been stealing all the coffee.
The head of HR sent out her accusations today.

No one has noticed our depleted rations
of baked beans, tinned spaghetti,
the dwindling four-litre bottles of water.
No one notices things like that
in the middle of a crisis situation.

Winter Swimmers

When the sky is monochrome,
the trees more yellow than green,
stacked like vertical cloud,
the puffed density of a storm,
this is when I think of trilobites,
their exoskeletons perfectly preserved,
three longitudinal lobes, pleural, axial,
scattered across the earth.

The first time I saw a trilobite
it was only a trace fossil,
tracks forming a dotted line
along ancient sea bed –
and then, there they were,
swimming along our salty sheets,
resting in our ancient sea bed,
showing us their soft body parts.
They were everywhere and nowhere.

I lie on my own elaborate spine
chanting for horseshoe crabs
to grow horns, two tails,
a trident from my forehead,
to form more complex eyes,
lenses, a stack of calcite prisms,
arranged hexagons
suitable for underwater living.

How many thousands of them
swimming in the Cambrian seas
five hundred million years away?

Sophie van Waardenberg

does a potato have a heart?

we are working on standing still

here is a photo of our arms
(and how they love each other
how their hands arrange themselves
as florists touching flowers
the turned-in child fingers
the raw adult knuckles
alternating closed and open orchids
one blunt fat elbow concaving a hawaiian shirt ribcage
one blunt fat elbow cradled in its grown-up other
in the good job love of tight holding not letting go
until the shutter closes)

unhatched egg/two girls at easter

we are helping to cut down the trees
they say. we know what the hills will look like
when we have finished. they will have burn scars
like we have on our wrists from clumsiness, from baking.
the dog tastes a hundred empty rabbit holes.
in a rooted place in the shadows in pine needles
we find our white egg, perfect, give it a name out of silence,
we share our hands over it, we pretend to love it
then slowly like it is a grenade I wrap it in my pink shirt.
the land rover rocks us, belimbs us onto gravel.
at the farmhouse I listen for a beat
before I let go to her. it carries on like this
and in darkness we drag our chairs across the rocks
to be close to the fire. we are gentle we think.
now that we have saved our bird we make plans for its first winter
and when it cracks
against my belly button I tell nobody, not for a night.
in the morning we two bury the fresh-cut shell by the river
where her parents had their honeymoon
and at hot noon with downy arms we swim there
under trees our failure has grown for us so quickly.

rocky shore

we were taught
radula, ventricle, neptune's necklace
and wondered why anything
would bother spending its life
with its tongue stuck to a rock.
imagine the charge of the light brigade
but with limpets.
imagine christmas ornaments
but limpets.
imagine if in a restaurant
they put limpet on the menu
and tried to make it sound like
something a knife and fork would
look beautiful opening.

red brick, stamford street

at eight thirty-eight when we skype our mothers
the sun has been down for days. and through cold lips
we talk all the way home about the supermarket fruit
how avocados from sainsbury's are always ready to eat.
we press toes against toes through cardboard walls.

so maybe the sun has not been down for days we say
but this is my longest night. we use the words we hardly use
except to our mothers. *thank you. scared.*
they pull our mouths back into shape.
and when only our mothers are looking we say look, here

here is the chain ripped from the anchor. look, here
are the leaving-home bruises, here
is where it hurts like my puzzle head is missing a piece.
life is good, I am lucky, I am cold and my walls are bare.
we are cold without mothers though at our age
we should keep ourselves warm. put some socks on.

can you hear the girl in room a?
if I kissed my bedroom walls, everyone
in the whole building would feel how bad I am at kissing.
the eight spoilt girls in apartment sixty-nine, we are not joking,
say, they all like their avocados wrong. one of them strips hers bare

all at once like she is peeling an egg
and another only eats hers pepperblack with a button of sunrise yolk
and another leaves her knife out green and wet on the kitchen table.
she leaves her sesame seeds on the lino, portents shivering at the open door
saying look, here, I told you there were ghosts.

at night when we tell our mothers of these london avocados
twins cradled in dark forest cardboard
we realise how odd we all are, how unfurnished, how children.
we show them the gum knotted into the carpet of our recycled bedrooms.
how nobody has quite cared for us. how we are home soon and past mattering.

I only took one photo of switzerland

is it still this morning we are living in
where we woke up with our single duvets pulled shut on us
hoping our skins to become soft by the cotton we wear?
it is difficult in three layers of clothing
to know where we sit on the globe.
having taken me so far without shutting your ears
you are my only friend.
you make the slick peeling of mandarin segments
sound affectionate. you give me the bigger half.
I am tired of talking to you
through the thick wool of my wordless love.
I make you slow with my bad stories. I make you slow
with my apologies. help me with my hat
and I will lend it to you soon
to keep the rain out of your hair
if you kiss me there
on that clean train station floor tomorrow
without phone reception – if you let me take your suitcase
though I will bruise it with my desperate care.
I want the best – and all for you – and what I can do at this dark table
is peel the white strings off the mandarin half
and nearly kindly feed what is left to myself.
it is still this morning and I don't know the shape
of switzerland but it must be like one of these pieces.

all the friendship bracelet makers have retreated

and now I'm not sure if I'm missing home
because I'm missing her or her
or just the sea. the sea is warming up
and I am jealous of all the toes it will kiss
before it kisses mine.

there is no ocean here. don't argue
that the river is in some way an ocean.
find a way to velcro us across the continents:
your arms hooking my winterburnt elbows.

I want to be far away but I want to be home.
breath by breath I want these things.
let me show you how little I want to know:
make a fist and let no air in.
I want to make the world as tight around me
as I make my single duvet in winter.

all the friendship bracelet makers have retreated.
they have gone home for the summer
to walk their dogs and recognise their parents
and I know I should stop sending photographs
of the same places but it is all I can do

to prove I am succeeding. watch me walk
chin-up through waterloo station
watch me rub mascara from my cheeks
wade through pigeons interrupt cyclists
listen to brahms on my crumbed carpet
and not even think of you.

to keep all the bees out

this love changes nothing, except now
    the house is covered in streamers
    there is no flavour in the cheesecake
and the geese we feed at western springs
    will ignore us on our bikes
    will thank us for our soft hands
and the election polls on friday nights
    somehow will make us dance
    like happy broken puppets
and the cherry blossoms we paint with our fingers
    will stay pink for decades
    will blame us for their smiles
and the hills we choose to climb
    are neither flat nor gently rolling
    are eaten by their own edges
and the right ventricle of the human heart
    does not have doors heavy enough
    to keep all the bees out, and their stings

apricot

plucked early
from the best tree in your novel
and rolled from hand to hand

quietly never ripening the sun
in your teeth tells herself a joke
and blushes

schön

my girl watered her cacti until they drowned
my girl filled my house with flowers until the house coughed and fell down

my girl ties yellow ribbons to my hair with her cold hands
and calls me beautiful in swooping german and my girl laughs

when my girl laughs she cuts my life in two and two again
where she kisses me there is love fizzing from my cheeks to the car windows

and we walk into the supermarket at midnight when the lilies have
     gone quiet
and hold hands past the eggs and milk and cut-price easter bunnies

when my girl wakes up she looks at me close and still smiles
my girl nearest to me in the world plucks her eyebrows and frowns and
     proves her face

my girl and I, here we are, refusing to decide what to feed each other
in the crumbed kitchen with the lights off

my girl and I spill our egg yolks on wednesday's astrology
forget that we are paper boats pushed out to sea by wistful hands

my girl forgets with me the drycleaning ticket
my girl forgets with me the breakfast cost

my girl becomes a calendar and I curl up inside her
my girl becomes a tongue twister and I curl up inside her

my girl lets the spring in through her hands
she puts her hands over my ears and I remember how it feels

it is nice and nice and nice

january at the bloemenmarkt

                                              I am melting

through the flower market   folding

neck and hands   around the few who bloom

                      in the snow.

                      all I want is to fall in

   the canal underfoot.   water runs faster than this air

            and you are not here and   I am wearing your socks.

am I doing it right?   on the wall seed packets:

            van gogh and sunny girl and happy generation

     blooming photographed   as if the sun is lit up now.

                            I cannot

figure out where my   body starts but the cheese

is grinning at me   from its pleasant window

across the street

                    and if there were time

   I would shoulder   through bicycles

to buy a yellow wheel   and call it yours.

         and if there were time I would

                        become beautiful here

shine so loud   you could hear me

                                       wherever.

complaint

sometimes I get cold when I think of your hands.
your hands are always cold when you walk in the door.
maybe it means you are dying. probably slowly that is true

but when you walk into our house I don't think of you dying –
instead that I wish you would be quieter when you shut the door,
and I wish you would turn the lock because it is dark when you walk in

and you make the cold so big around you. you make such a season of it all,
like it is your stop and you alone have to leave the bus
through its ringing jaws into the wind.

somehow you are sweetcurved in my mind but in my arms a lesson of
      polygons.
maybe it is my fault. maybe I have worn the hills of your voice flat with my
      wide feet.
but I am not sorry. you are for me. should I say things like this?

we have walked too long together, around the same block, the same strangers,
you too fast, I too slow, and always too seriously.
you read too much into my badly written face.

when we are on the phone together there is not much to share.
on your end, wind in the valley of wherever you always are,
on my end, only frost and skyscrapers.

I am things you will never understand: slow, unsteady, full of maybe.
I am watery blue against your ochre and my waist is wider but I don't want
      to change.
I am bread and you are roses, or the other way, or are we too much of
      each other?

look at all the breath I have for you!
look at all the breath you waste of me!
I cannot decide which way to love you.

do not blame me for loving the 2003 film love, actually

because it should snow
all the dogs should wear stupid shoes
noses are beautiful
at christmas when you are in love
even when you are a grown man
a body double in a porn film
airports are beautiful
if you don't cry –
the beach boys at heathrow
and people in love immediately again
– you are not worthy to criticise
even the planes hold hands
between their gates
though this does not happen and the flowers
wilt from changing arms I know I am wrong
colin firth and bill nighy and emma thompson
should make better art
snow does not look like that
body doubles probably do not fall in love
you cannot blame me it is maths
to like the 2003 film love,
actually
an idiot in a cold street
unfairly criticised pie
a lobster in a nativity
every possible demonstration of easy emotion
nipples censored by christmas hats
sometimes
we like bad films just like sometimes
we choose bad poems
to read at christenings
and the funerals of loyal pets
and later we are embarrassed
they belong in cross-stitch
in hospital waiting rooms

instead pin them to our child hearts
that love whatever they feel
sometimes the things that hurt shouldn't hurt too much
love like snow shouldn't care
if you can't speak its language
should fall you into it anyway

if you cannot draw good pictures

cut off the hands of the parent you can't remember
and then maybe you'll remember him – how
in the evenings he would stretch, close
the door behind him, jog into the trees in shorts
from the eighties. cut off his feet and by making less
recall more. the tradescantia flower tonguing his nose
as he knelt to kill it and the mosquitoes always
angering above the elbow. place a new sheet
of paper over the face you cannot build
and you might understand how the heart worked,
how it slipped your brother, your mother, your aunts,
the clumsy botany, the kind and the wrong,
the robbed grey ford at cornwallis, and
the you inside it like salty liquorice snatched
and saved for later. draw a line from his shoulder
to his shoulder and maybe he will stand up straight,
empty his pockets of lint and sleep, take you in.

it is only the morning

you find your mother
on the kitchen floor –
her phone on the bench
under flour reciting bach
some distance from her ear.
she's fine and you know it –
a hand caught on the handle
of the drawer of spoons.
you must broaden your ideas
as to what a melody may be.
last night a super blue blood moon
dropped into your hands from
somewhere above. silent
and rough – you felt proud
to hold it. it asked for nothing.
pick your mother up – the beats
of her feet contrapuntal –
the butter on the wrong knife
shining painlessly. see see
the word is incarnate the birds
in the chimney have woken up –
their feathers are falling off –
don't worry. you can't help them.

this is a coping mechanism

seven years later in unfairness
I stand holding flowers

for someone else
on an empty driveway

while the trees drip.
I am turning this lack

into leaves, thick
and veined like muscles

lifting heavy things.
this is a coping mechanism

from my worksheet.
the leaves grow out of my heart

or somewhere.
my dress is damp with autumn.

my eyes are not wet.
my eyes are not wet.

I have finished with sadness.
I am foliage now.

all growing, all well.

I don't remember inviting you

my body is seven rows of empty chairs
and you are at the front, boring me legless.
be offended, or don't. every single face of mine
is a safe harbour. every single face of mine is blank.

my body is made out of several kinds of metal
and you are trying to warm it with your small limbs.
breakable. my body is the bone scanner. it is the guest
in your skeleton that alarms you into every country.

go away, well well away, take yourself through my doors
and back into the sun. my body has had its funding cut
and is making you redundant. be offended, or don't. fly
to france, to california. tell me about it abstractly. wonder

at your luck. my body has a space inside it.
a big space inside it. there it is clean and loud. soon
it will be full of pigeons like piazza san marco.
nobody will be taking any pictures. but you

unfortunately pam beesly I fell in love with you briefly

by which I mean
your season-one hair is the easy life I long for.
it is clear to me for one second that I love you,

by which I mean
you are a driverless van full of flowers.
it is always, isn't it, the boy with the stupid hair
with the nose like a good and hopeful christmas ornament
who looks at you nicely and points you
in just the right direction

by which I mean
if I do not love something I do not remember it.

by which I mean
if I love something I do not watch it only once,
but over again, looking to the corner of the room,
the reception desk, you in the chair, tinselbright,
waiting for love to fit itself over you
like a jumper.

by which I mean
five episodes are enough to know I am enough in love
to reverse out of the warehouse and down the street
and into anyone's wedding, destroying the ceremony,
the whole cake. pam beesly, I'm bored of you

by which I mean
it's not your fault but mine
for wanting too little, wanting to choose
an uncomplicated and unstoried love: never
a statement and only a light, one light of many lights
like in the christmas episode you never film
with the tree that is real and decorated perfectly.

notes on the girls with the red cardigans

in the café out of the wind
I am eating stale pie, and
they are eating stale pie.
we are trying to eat it.

> *there are no more good words*
> *to name your band.*
> *just the bad words left,*
> *like … malcolm.*

pie is flying everywhere,
from their four forks and my fork.
pie is resting at my two feet,
their eight feet, sandalled.

> *oh, you're taking it with you?*
> *do you need a bag?*
> *oh, you're carrying it*
> *in your hands like that?*

pink fruit is wanting in our mouths
– young, I'm young, know nothing except
the sugar of the endless afternoon
the endless afternoon of late winter

> *do you think that there's*
> *an earthquake and*
> *there's no budget?*
> *there's always a budget.*

treading raspberries into the cracked footpath
that leads away from the school. I am following it
chewing lonely laughter like hard crust.
the shoes would still fit if I tried them on.

does a potato have a heart?

it's not that I mind about hurting. I just wonder about the anatomy.

when I cut into blank flesh do I nick the aorta?

unstarch my fingers in the kitchen sink and forgive me. at fifteen

we named our locust before we sliced him. and even though

we were meant to see how he breathed we did not see anything,

only inside, which was now everywhere. were we ever sorry –

I don't think so. on my favourite cooking show they are always saying

you must respect the cut of meat. you must let it rest. that is a very expensive

failure. that is a very expensive sauce. we cannot eat that, and so

you are going home. the cooks on my favourite cooking show have big faces

and they never want to go home, even though their children . . . when I am
    grown up

I will respect the world and everything in it. I will julienne my carrots,

I will learn to trust celery, raisins, prawns. I will cut with love

everything in my garden so that it grows again.

agape

on the south bank I tie
my light to your balloon
and we let it go, our hands like mouths

yawning. this is spring:
the sweet shops are open wide.
their doors warm in the sun.

we are brightly wrongly dressed
pretending on our semi-detached feet
to know what it is to walk

through trafalgar square without losing.
your almost kiss on my shoulder is a pink flag
still. I will hold ten years

to the palace gate, my acrylic arm
bright on the gilded bar
ready for your disposable.

grace wakes late

and I don't have anything to say. and in the morning, all sentences
dulled by light, the chives stand shocked, they grow every day.

                                                                             I worry
for you because you are worried, the week is big, the milk is bad, the future
is staring at you

                as if you have an answer for it. you should. grace
appears like a teaspoon when you have run out of teaspoons,

                                                                               dips
into your coffee, into your mouth. there are things I cannot do for you.

when you are grown you drink coffee. I am not grown. I am a small hum,
a joke and a song, I don't know how to make good the milk –

                                                                  you must go,
grace in your buttons and gold, with your handfuls and handfuls of music,
your handfuls and handfuls, handfuls and handfuls,

                                                                       so much
that there are no commas left to organise you. and it is always time to go.

Rebecca Hawkes

Softcore coldsores

Primal scream practice

This is the beginning of language   A planet
huge and awful throwing itself at the nearest star
and missing   Water gnawing toothlessly at the land
Birds screaming territory borders   People
baring their teeth in glee   *The beginning
of language*   in a bar   being touched
by strangers   like an animal at a petting zoo   *The language of*
Knowing   the closest I can come to winning the lottery
is seeing my suitcase come first around the airport conveyor belt
The beginning of   When you look at me
and do not know I can see you looking   you seem
so disappointed
Teach me   how to prize what is of value   *The beginning
of language*   Begging   You   cradling me   flushed
like a $25.99/kg slab of salmon fresh and pungent in your hands
my tongue erodes you like the tide   I want   You want
for me to sweatily slip anchor here and stay   but
I cannot make my home in you   I need a place
we all need   a place that is not inside of anyone else
This is the beginning of language   I am eating
a ham and coleslaw sandwich so enormous that I have to
hold it with both hands   but so far nothing has fallen
out of it   This makes me feel powerful
To hold something   and have it not fall apart

Gremlin in sundress

blinded with dandelion gimme a puff of it
gimme an eyelash kiss gimme ringlets
gimme a morsel of raw
vegan cheesecake gimme this day
my daily bliss gimme the creamy
origami of the rose and the honeybee
scritching in her folds gimme sickled
tarsus to whet against latent ovary gimme
pollen somersault buzzy gimme gingerbeer
low alcohol but not no alcohol
you know gimme recreational
toxins and parlour games gimme electrolyte
saltwater to chug like chamomile tea
as you tuck me in gimme bedtime gimme curfew
to flout gimme a truant insolence
and let me call it bravery call me
yer hungerling gimme a gobble
of the pantry gimme soft-shelled sweetmeat
gimme something pretty but with brains
I can crack open gimme salt'n'pepper
tentacle dredged from the abyss and deep
fried gimme hot cephalopod gimme yer cold
shoulder gimme yer murmuring
muffled against my nerve endings
gimme yer tenderness gimme cheesy fries
gimme drunkenness gimme the vomitorium
next door to the buffet gimme mortal clay
with tingle and baby fat to live in
gimme glory gimme eternity gimme yer likings
to make me yer favouritest gimme
a cute burial gimme my own museum
exhibit with a tame scorpion
glowing under ultraviolets gimme violent light
on yer body gimme martyrdom
and scurvy gimme divinity I want all of it nonstop

Dairy queen

you're the other shedhand on the early milking shift
and you work shirtless
under your heavy rubber apron
which I appreciate from behind –
muscles moving under your tan
perspiring   glossy as a cold can of golden pash
         unfortunately the overall effect is ruined
       by your bleach-blonde dreadlocks   Grinch fingers
      dyed greenish by weeks of cowpat splashback

the splatter of digested turnip this morning has a smell so strong I can hear it
as though my teeth are thirty crystal glasses and somebody
is tracing a finger along them
with skill and ease   maybe   dear colleague   this could be you
     oh when will you snap off your latex gloves and   oblige me

   nobody would hear us
over the rhythmic chug of teat pumps with their fake baby suck
     musical lactation Fleshlights syncopated with radio blare
    Lana Del Rey wailing
     her popular summertime sadness
I am troubled that some sadnesses are more adorable than others
I am tired of loving people for theirs
I resent asking to be loved in spite of mine
   all summer
   I've been skittish   and gentle   like a puppy
    saying hello by resting my whole mouth around your hand but not biting

this is the only responsible form of tenderness –
     hands limp with trust in each other's mouths
   but practising secret reflexes just in case
fangs clamp sharp   don't call it cynical
even though we are all secretly untrustworthy I still advocate for getting
   vulnerable
particularly when I'm 4am shift delirious
     highly caffeinated   ripe with morning

through a slit in the corrugated iron
the moon is bright pumice   bobbing in a darkness bathtub
I want to shuck off my gumboots and scrub my feet on it

I want to climb into the feed troughs while you pull the chute
so I am bathed in barley seed and spurts of molasses
it would be the gushiest ever
        the cows could lick me clean

        we milk the sick girls last
their udders so sore and swollen with mastitis that they jog pendulously
to their places by the milking cups to hurry us
              their milk comes out mixed with blood
              the safe lurid pink of a strawberry milkshake
frothing into a bucket
it looks so gross
        but so sweet

The flexitarian

I am trying to go vegetarian but finding myself weak,
week to week browsing the meat aisle at a linger
close enough to chill my arms to gooseflesh. I only buy
stuff so processed it hardly makes sense to call it meat.
Saveloy, nugget, continental frankfurter;
whatever gets extruded pink beyond possible memory
of the preceding body. Between the red and yellow flags
delineating the PORK section, I fondle sheets
of pig skin through their clingfilm. Flaps of fat and dermis,
bloodless as the nude silicone on a sex doll. Sad rubber
reanimates in the oven. Whimpering fat
melts to breathless squeal. The grill huffs,
fogs my glasses like hot breath. Like kissing
someone else's boyfriend right outside her flat in winter.
Sometimes the pig has not been properly shaved. Needle
hairs prick my lips. Sometimes draw blood. Sometimes red
ink from the slaughterhouse is printed on the sallow skin.
Lipstick; damp napkin. The worst possible outcome
is unfurling the limpid rind from its plastic tray only to find
a nipple tucked inside. I try to cut it out but no knife
in my house is sharp enough. The nipple stares
a pert pink accusation. It follows me around the room.
I score the skin, scrub it raw with salt and rapeseed oil.
The nipple winks at me. Weeps in the pan as it shrinks
to helpless hiss and spit. The crackling bubbles
perfectly crisp. Blisters where I burn my tongue on it.

Would I recognise the garden if I saw it

why would you come here with me willingly when
this is exactly how horror movies start –
panting up a sunless path somewhere
deciduous where the trees are darker than the night sky
and not for surplus of stars – O the stink
of rotting fly agaric and soggy earth –
maybe you're actually into it or maybe you're just being polite
          precarious on your edge of the wooden raft
          which is parked in the clearing like an altar

until we're all out of chardonnay and ready salted chips
and somehow into a fumbling
of nuzzled permissions – inhaling my own rank breath
from the yielding socket of your neck –
wet air rancid as a shearing shed
wafting ammonia and lanolin –
black pearls of shit rattling down the chutes
before the shorn yearlings are chucked through – I
       don't know how to talk to you
     or if I am interesting enough to love
now I've gone and got myself buried in your mouth

– engraved in it –

this bafflement of teeth and excess nerve endings
like – licking nectarine honey off a paring knife
    – sweetness pierces the tongue like a staplegun
   like a shaft of light
zeroed convex to burning point
through a magnifying glass held
over some unfortunate ant – wrong
place wrong time and so highly combustible
– I find myself wanting

                 wrong things – bite until I burst every capillary
all over you to bruise – the smell of your skin hairs shrivelling to ash
too close to a source of intense heat – I don't know why I ache after
what is most hurtful – as though I could skin everyone who is nice to me
and live inside of them – is there anything
I react to more violently than gentleness – it's just
                                 – there's a lot going on right now

vagrant heart brandishing its amnesias
like a cellphone torch to light the way
and laughing at our stumble up the slick clay incline
– can we lie down – can I leave my shoes on – in a kind of redness
inflammatory and luxuriant as the indefensible
pop songs of our youth – crooked fingers
bucking on the way to somewhere
                         unspecified by language

and then a falling branch in the dark
a body
crying out and trembling beneath mine

The cave draws you in like a breath

walls corrugated like the cartilaginous ribbing of a trachea
& just as wet   algaed slick muculent

the limestone bedrock vivisected
by years   a hairline fissure concedes
to cavernous lack   this sanctuary of emptiness

you yield to it   spelunking
                       perhaps
                               you are in love
you are not in love   you are in a cave
a reassurance of creamy calcite catacombing you amid its fossils
clamp your parts bivalve or whorl yourself gastropod
whatever it takes to get some   stillness
         from what's inside you
you merciless you selfish unfurling your fervency
in nobody's cathedral
                these crumpled aeons of shell
                forgetting the shapes they once held

& how much can you bend to fit the whittled geometry of a fondness
        which turns your interior to delicate meat   a mollusc
          & are you prepared   to petrify like that
                   cinched long after the tender flesh desiccates
o soft salt heart so edible
dare you opalise for this?

hopping from stone to stone when slipshod you plunge
your accidental sole into the water

                the cave chokes on you

heaves   its echoes of life

you are going so deep so quickly
you are losing the light

Cold speculum

I anchor my eyes away from him, mooring myself in the blue
of a rubber glove balled up in the rubbish bin. Knees open,

all anticipation, but still shocked by the chill of prising.
Newly aware of all the acts of care I never notice

until they're missing: prongs warmed in a latex-clad hand
or a light brush of inner thigh in vectored warning,

the way one would rest a courteous hand on a mare's rump
so as not to startle when manoeuvring behind her.

Does he think I won't kick? Is he Catholic or something?
Trying not to be gentle with me as though any implication of tenderness

could make this barely lubricated glowstick somehow sexy?
Even though it's so far from those short weeks ago with you

when we smelled the rain before we could see it, and
heady petrichor rose while a distant cloud unspooled

its load over the alpine fault. Those rough tectonics,
plates grinding up and down the islands all upthrust and subduction

plus us, unregistered by the Richter scale, quaking
our campground while the sea sucked off the rocks

and the sky bloomed just like the suckled bruise
on a neck, or all my credible fears, blossoming

under my belly to cast roots there, bulbous
as pickling onions, marinating a promise

neither intended to keep. Hence this more perfunctory affair.
You: God-knows-where. Me: gritting my teeth to dilation

under a roof gridded with tiles like an upturned swimming pool.
I wish we could do this outside. I would rather look up at the sky

and its well-aerated blue so contrary to drowning, although
I would still be holding my breath

wishing I could get engulfed in something
rather than doing all the damn engulfing.

Add penetrant to preferred broadleaf herbicide
& devastate the wildflowers

//   an overabundance of lupins scours the Mackenzie Country
scorched pestilent amid shallow rabbit digs & wildling pines
glacial sediment pigmenting lakes   blue as the cyanide-
spiked bliss balls we cull wallabies with
Ferafeed 217: Peanut Butter Classic
                              local farmers are obligated
to eliminate the lupins although a few plant them on purpose   contentiously
providing forage fodder for merino sheep in the high country
they're pretty   these weeds
deep rooted & pernicious   shedding
protein rich seeds & a kind of shade that only other unwanteds can live beneath

//   in a car park on the shore of Lake Tekapo
           the rabbit gets shot over & over again
           yet will not die

a squad of amateur photographers lined up
                  as the rabbit hustles into the lupin thicket

           where I crouch low unspotted by the throng
                              their lanyards & itineraries
           to snap up unpopulated scenery
           in a picture I will not send you
snow-capped peaks etcetera   & of course the noxious pastel tapestry
                              a cheap pixelated sunset
                              an aestheticised bruise
plus a rabbit that poses for me like warm taxidermy
     half the sun cupped in its silky earlobe
     blood vessels ignited petal pink

    I expect the photo could win an award at the A&P show
    if they hadn't banned pictures of the stupid lupins
                  the lazy ease
                            of such inconsiderate loveliness

  the tour bus moves on   the rabbit & I remain

//
                  all humanity's accomplishments
                  are due to a six-inch layer of topsoil
                  & the fact that it rains

//
      where it won't rain we irrigate
                      until the green believes us
crop circles patrolled by centre pivots
      unparching the lucerne   the clover   *Hieracium*
          this false precipitation this sunshower of effluent
rainbows glinting from the fine spray of shit

//
so much depends on
      whether the sheep are hungry enough
            to tolerate the taste of toxic alkaloids

as the lupins bloom out the summer in their splendid blushing colonies
    both the planters of lupins & their weedkiller neighbours insist
    that nature should take its course
           but they can't agree on what nature means:
conserving shrivelled unpalatable tussock or letting slip
the lupine war on the landscape   floral battalions

whose thorns do you prefer
sweet briar rosehip or matagouri

//
                the lupins lend their purpleness to prose & I
am ill equipped   to be alone
      with this sentimental glut
      unearned emotions   a   too-easy picturesque
      florid & fecund & phallic   all guzzle & loll
      choking the riverbed with sex
ovaries & stamens   orbicular pods   naked waxen stems
      little pink hoods yielding   like skin inside out
      fallow on linens which still reek   of cross-pollination
                                      I suppose you could say
I haven't buried the hatchet   I am still swinging it
in my splintered fist   I am building a tiny house with it in the Mackenzie
        Country
because I cannot live inside you

//
meanwhile the lupins   wring out their bright disaster of seeds
in the riverbed   & propagate downstream

The land without teeth

the year my body learns about want
I wake with hunger before the dawn
& rummage stale raisins from the muesli box

I suck them until the grapes rehydrate enough to denude
from their tasteless skins with my tongue   it makes them last
I pocket five withered fruits as though that breaks the fast

I whistle the dogs to me from their kennels
ready for ascension in corduroy & gumboot
& scuff through hoarfrost to the bush gate

up a route I take every morning in the hours before light
early riser clambering the crest of the mountain
away from the family home   the little cat warming my bed

the taunting kitchen   I come here
to get back to the stone that made me
to escape my mulchsoft body   returning

to the old volcano's swollen belly
fleshpink rhyolite muscular with its red web of veins
like mine   thinblood anaemic   red knees skinned on the rock

crumbling iron &   crystalline structures
walking the dogs up the mountain in the dark
& stumbling my malnourishment but oh the sunrise

gilding the frost   fenceposts polished to silverware
the light so cold & loud it clangs like a cutlery drawer in anger
my pores whorl open into spiracles that gasp for extra air

becoming so unbodied   I sublimate
I get with the dirt
dizzy with cold & lightness I

am the black beech & the red tussock & filigree
lichen I'm honeydew I'm
braided into silver ribs

like the river below oh no I'm
more slender than a harebell stem
that can hardly hold up its pale head   five petals

bluelipped   but this body's no alpine native
don't mistake me for some mystic nationalist
in my whiteness   & my rhetoric of wilderness

I am introduced to this place
like the gravel track tattooed on the slopes
& the unstrung barbed wire

spangled with needlefrost
I am   the pregnant heifer gouging out the valley
for fear of the dogs that chased her there

& I'm the dogs laughing for meat I'm buttery
gorsebloom yes I'm that
impregnable alien

pricklebitch skeleton
asway underneath my nodding
marzipan-scented yellows

forbidden stellated spindle I could rag you like plasticbag
all claw & fang   tell me I am your favourite coloniser
besides you couldn't unroot me if you tried

which I would know   I try so
hard my seeds lie dormant
still   I'm evergreen

me & my entire invasive species
consuming this landscape once so toothless
its homely fatbirds plumped defenceless in the shrubcover

where my little cat   collarless   devours them
with malice   leaves them gutted in my bed
as though I need a reminder of bones

Tropical snow

All summer we dragged those bodies around that wanted nothing to do with us. Our bodies told us what they thought they needed, and we had no choice but to listen. The bodies blew eggs and filled their painted shells with shots of liquor. The bodies could have sworn a DJ stopped the remix to whisper 'I'm sad' into the mic before resuming his sick beats, dropping some of the hottest hits of the '80s. Later, in that same heaving discotheque, somebody had to peel the leftover synonyms for desire off the bathroom floor. We have since abandoned those insatiable bodies – we managed it either by sheer force of will or total lack of attention. It was the freest season, but also the heaviest.

Barbecue mirage

The national meringue sweats under its clingfilm,
pavlova leaking beads of honey like my cracked lips
where the coldsore crust has split
and weeps me salted syrup. The afternoon
pulses with perhaps. A headache
glitters in my lobes. I water it down
with a dose of sparkling sav. Pour one out for the baby
who today belongs to. Covertly bunch
my dress into my underwire and mop up
the underboob humidity. We are approaching
peak pōhutukawa. Massed stamens bristle
for a tickle of bees, flaring
their festive threads incarnadine. You
must be thirsty. You're looking at me
across the laden trestle table
as though I am a cup that never empties.
All my relatives keep saying
my life is going to change.
They nod seriously to demonstrate
their depth of sympathy. When you
thud down your spent beer bottle
the table bows like a donkey kneeling
towards me, delivering
the pav into my lap. Its gentle soak
of sweet cream creeps
up my thigh
and makes my skirt go
see-through.

If I could breed your cultivar I'd have you in my garden

I gripped your hand white-knuckled
as we scuffed through beefy snowdrifts –
dead magnolia blossom

heaped on the pavement
bride-pale & fragrant & going so greasy
underfoot you slipped. I caught you

at the elbow – not so much to right you
as to encourage you to fall
into me. But you fixed yourself

& said, that was close.
The blush raged across my body
like a barbarian horde

torching everywhere it passed through.
Because you were a fantasy
I had certain expectations –

grab me by my hair, drag me
to your lair & do your worst
etceteras. We had the scenery for it –

a backdrop of unmeltable snow.
Snow that only bruised
without healing. Petal perfume turning

necrotic like the breath of a meat-eater,
retchworthy but I kind of wanted it.
Waiting for another gust in my face

to make certain my disgust was legitimate. Sorry
but could I pluck out that muscle flapping loose
in your mouth? Another slimy petal

windblown & useless. I preferred you
quiet as a magnolia cutting, propped
in a jar & dreaming up the tree you could be.

Technicolour dreamcake

well now I must admit to painting you
in an unsayably saturated light

pre-raphaelite nymphknave incendiary
knelt among wildflowers

bulging with significance
souped up from the loam

swaddled in kerosene fragrance
I yield to pheromone and accident

between our fluorescent camo and exposed roots
we can only guess what moths might flock to us

Meanwhile

you wake up. your grandfather
is telling you that your generation is too dependent
on technology. 'no *your* generation is too
dependent on technology' you retort and you pull out the plug
on his life support to make sure he gets it. *you wake up.*
in class you put your hand up for questions
but you are always compelled to begin your answer with 'sorry'.
you wake up. you are fishing with your father.
you are secretly repulsed by the things he enjoys.
you watch the eels sliming their slow-motion
ribbon dance while he meticulously oversees
the unspooling of fish guts back into the water. *you wake up.*
your skin is slippery with sweat
under the plaster cast. you want to scratch it
but you can't. you can't move. *you wake up.*
you lie on the bed unmoving. the nubs of bone
have finally begun to crack their way through the skin on your forehead.
your lover comes in and stares at you from the doorway.
there is much biting of lips.
in a month when your antlers have fully formed
you stand at the edge of the forest. watch your lover from the trees
as they stare into the sun from the porch
before rubbing their eyes harder than is necessary.
they wipe their hands on their shirt and lock the door
when they go back inside. you bend down your graceful neck
to chew the sweet young grass.
you wake up. you are a bad dog
and the person you love the most in the world
is holding a gun to your forehead. the ring of metal
is cold. there is a tremble to it. your questionless trust
absolves you of all responsibility. *you wake up.*
it is not your fault for not running.
you wake up. you wonder can a heart still be heavy
when it's empty. you imagine yours in the shape of a tooth. a shell
of white enamel, rotted from the root. it looks okay

but there's nothing inside except glutinous residue
and an upsetting smell. you find it difficult
to bite down hard on anything these days. *you wake up.*
you've had your wisdom teeth pulled out
and your cheeks have swollen around the absence of bone there.
the itchy ends of the stitches wiggle
and shred against a part of your tongue that is not used to being touched.
every time you swallow there's a little bit of blood going down.

Grooming

    i.

Mother says 'sit' so Werewolf sits. Everyone forgets
the distance between wolves and humans
and where halfway is met. The domesticated median of *dog*.
Werewolf couldn't disobey if she wanted to, any more than resist
pouncing for a frisbee at the peak of its parabola or fetching
thrown sticks. It's been worse since she hit puberty.
Not only more hirsute but the jokes about shag carpet
and bitches have taken on a more urgent tone.
Somehow all her classmates know
that when someone says 'bad girl'
with calm admonition, Werewolf cowers. Begins to fold
inside herself like a rubber glove unrolled from a vet's hand
she knows she is supposed to shake.

    ii.

  good girl
Werewolf whines, kicks her school shoes against the metal legs
perched on the stool on the porch in the meek winter sun
and Mother fires up the electric razor. This is their ritual
during the waxing moon. Werewolf's morning bath, luxuriant
full-body lather, razoring herself naked as the cloudless day
and then her mother fussing on the balcony
to shave the dense mane tufting from her
shoulders, her back, the contours of her face.
  so very good
Cool blades kiss her brow. Werewolf snuffs in a tickle of trimmings
and Mother's own smells – gentle dandruff shampoo,
deodorant caked armpit, peach and mango yoghurt, breakfast tea.
She closes her eyes and leans into the world of odour, begins to groan
and dribble for the very interesting scents coming from the neighbours' garbage
until she smells the fear rise sour in her mother

> *a good girl good please*

Werewolf looks up at Mother pleading and loyal.
The sun shines Werewolf's hair dry
and glints four times.
Mother's open scissors.
Daughter's open eyes.
> *a good girl she's good she's good she's trying so hard to be*

But the hair grows back overnight
like the promise of ferocity, those lengthening canines
> *good girl*

Werewolf clutches her muzzle and grinds her teeth to blunting.

iii.

Werewolf lopes to the bus stop with her lunchbox of rare steak
and Mother sweeps soft curls from the veranda, scoops wet thickets
of hair from the bathtub, fills a black rubbish bag,
which she slings into her room
onto a pile of others like it, spilling over
the cold side of the bed. The damp
brackish smell of her daughter infuses the room.
Why would she keep all this?
How could she throw it away?

Overladen trellis

it's true   you never could bring yourself to prune
all these Icarus vines   grasping at the closest star
only to collapse with the weight of their reaching

sweetpea, wisteria, adventurous rose

rappelling on thorns that hitch sky to dirt
& snag shreds of you: polyester, keratin, ichor

birds collect snarls of your hair from the barbs
they build a nest from your loss   you don't notice
how many rely on you for shelter

even in your own home
breathing alone on your bare mattress   you slough
cell dust: the same plentiful gusts

as puffball spore, urchin sperm, pollen from shaken anther

spawning from your skin   a feast for mites
without even trying you satiate empires

and that's without even mentioning your microbiome

see how useful you are
as your body decays around you

how necessary

even in your lighthouse
up all those stairs

Death by nectar

Oh no
the mood for you
shudders through me
like an insect's glitching
  symphony for too many limbs
    drowning for purchase
      in the pitcher pit

Oh no
the sugar secretes
its sneaky enzymes and I
 am fizz become elixir
 hey eater be eaten
dissolving mouthparts first
consumed by my own hunger I
  must wonder if you love
    me every moment

Oh no
I must close the lid on my crawling
body restless for this honeytrap gullet
these speckles of red and green shrieking
 stop and go at the same time
  as I surrender to syrup I
   must pray the pitcher
    withers on its stalk
     before I
       disintegrate
         entirely

Shield your eyes for the bright of it

at dusk we paddle sultry in the mangrove
caress each other's unshaved calves for leeches
engorged & drunk on us
until at distant brackish splash your bullet cartridge pops like jewelweed
disturbing salamanders crawling upstream to spawn

oh please lay down your arms
raise your spinneret   your sting   your fruiting vine
welcome to my wetlands   my mucous   honeytrap glisten
like drosera sundew my kiss
is meant to keep

please stay   in my clutches
see: mayfly see: luna moth   with no parts for feeding
they are of single purpose   do you still have a mouth
show me its functions   its gag reflex
its needy congregation of teeth   show me your selfish
motivations

your useless methodologies   your broken   instruments
let us speculate   in this kaleidoscope of genders & colours
new applications of defunct machinery
see: grenade see: pomegranate
seeding kind rednesses

let us burrow toward that fractal spot & see
how quickly we disintegrate & mingle
our bodies a möbius strip   refracting our spectres please
see: me   transfixed by this glitter rimmed
geode   & the sheen over your eyelids

now blindfold   now swirling mercury
now skin velveteen with silver down like a protea petal
see: nectarivorous sugarbird easing its bill into the inflorescence
wantonly pollinating
lyrebird mimics the wildlife reporter narrating

a series of interspecies symbioses
life lusts for more of itself so urgently
oh darling let me inside your shimmering
get our extremities oil slicked & let them shift like liquid
am I you   are you me

all encounters fundamentally autoerotic
when my organs understand themselves through yours
saying who is the tunnel   & who is the tower today
& how do they glow
how do they go up in flames

Biologist abandoned

I lay in our bed all morning
next to the half-glass of juice you brought me
to sweeten your leaving

ochre sediments settled in the liquid
a thin dusty film formed on the meniscus

but eventually I drank it
siphoning pulp
through my teeth like a baleen whale sifting krill from brine

for months after your departure I refused to look at the moon
where it loomed in the sky outside

just some huge rude dinner plate you left unwashed
now ascendant
brilliant with bioluminescent mould

how dare you rhapsodise my loneliness into orbit
I laughed
enraged

to the thought of us
halfway across the planet staring up
at some self-same moon & pining for each other

but now I long for a fixed point between us
because from here
even the moon is different

unlatched
from its usual arc & butchered
by grievous rainbows

celestial ceramic irreparably splintered
as though thrown there
and all you have left me with
is this gift of white phosphorous

dissolving the body I knew you in
beyond apology
to lunar dust

Any machine can be a smoke machine if you use it wrong enough

Circe likes to live comfortably. The island,
the private jet – does putting everyone else
between Scylla and Charybdis make this
worth less? Hardly. Circe is moulding you
in her fingers like soft wax – here, amorphous

child of Morpheus, are you comfortable? Circe
takes her tax, she is a circular saw coaxing sap from a slack veiny tree
and in her menagerie the sad lion is left to starve
and chew his stately mane for comfort. She will destroy your planet
to live comfortably, but O! she is compelling –

for instance, she claims she's only anti-vaccination
insofar as she is against the continuation of the existence
of this human race, the world's worst disease, abominations
bombing nations, laughing lesions of senseless flesh celebrating
their own unsubtlety, the syrupy pus of which

she collects in a glass and holds to her lips. Bemused charmer
of every snake, she has taken men to space and yet has not succeeded
in getting them to respect it. She has fought a thousand wars for you
and your right to say that war is bad, although there is a comfort in it.
Knowing who your enemy is. Circe leaves a thick slick of spit

on the panther's taut haunch, sends him off with a resounding slap
and when his whispering ear is gone she advises you sincerely
to cultivate your loneliness, make your silence
violent, remember 'a woman's first blood doesn't come
from between her legs but from biting her tongue'. Circe says

to treat comfort ephemerally, like a fleecy faery-circle
of ringworm on the skin of your inner thigh, a sick unscratchable itch
you don't want to reach for. If you admit that you need something that badly
then it can be taken away from you. Circe instructs you to become blood
diamond, smoky topaz, hard-edged undesiring object of destructiveness

and self-destruction internalised by all as desire, as comfort, as Circe's white
dandelion-floss cat who flows down the street on his way to eat
or sleep or fornicate with the mouse he doesn't keep at home
instead silently stealing out to play with her
garnet heart among the liquorice-scented ferns.

Crush

venturing with my posse of apostates and mercenaries I find the golem in a field failing to scare corvids from the barley / the townsfolk say if I can move it I can take it

I survey my hulking metamorphic odalisque / mantled in guano / my golem strikes a thousand-year pose / clenching their cold knuckles to punch space vacated by a forgotten war

a fresh clutch of eggs shelter in the clumsy pit of the golem's ear / on the crude lobes of which I trace fingerprints / relics of the long-dead priests who pressed and pinched this raw clay anthropomorphic

respectfully I scrape off the crust of lichen and pigeon droppings / reactivate the golem with a whisper of the right words / and the assistance of a magic wand conveniently located in a nearby cavern

my golem shudders animate / splendid as a waking volcano / sneezing feathers and bird shit

complaining of however many centuries / of chirp and caw and caked cloaca dribbles

their voice is slow as lava / I feel it pool hot in my stomach / and settle there

I learn this golem desires nothing except to serve their master / and to never again suffer another bird

I ask their name and they make an unpronounceable sound / like the curdling clink of cooling obsidian / so I call them the ultimate war machine / they hurl rocks into my enemies and when they beat the earth with their fists / I feel the world quake under me / this is how I know I have fallen in love / but also onto the ground

their hollow eyes glow righteously / with the holy texts searing in the cavity behind their face / I so want them to like me

on the anniversary of their awakening I choose them the worst possible gift / the winking merchant promises hours of fun for the sky-rat hater in my life / so I buy the uncrushable pigeon

as planned I open the cage and the pigeon alights upon the golem / they clap the bird between clay fists then open their hands / to inspect pancaked grey down matted with gore glisten / the ultimate war machine's stone face doesn't move / but I almost see new cracks smirk satisfaction

only to watch the uncrushable pigeon unfurl from flattened / to bob and coo in their hands and resume its pecking / at the innermost crevices of the ultimate war machine's palms / parts of them even I cannot touch / because they will pulp me with one glittering micaceous clench

despite a series of painful and increasingly inventive deaths / the pigeon will not leave / we depart in the night while it sleeps / its homing senses lead it back to the golem / they are so magnetic / hematite veined

in light of my faults / the golem's esteem of me plummets to hostility

I have to etch new glyphs onto their iron collar to keep them with me / but even in homunculoid compliance they're all stomp and bellow / the comely hunch of craggy shoulders somehow flintier / serrated edges glint from each new fracture against pacification

I ask the ultimate war machine the name of the God that made them / they say they do not recall

I begin filling in their fissures with crystals from our quests / chipped amethyst raw emerald citrine like frozen honey / quartz whiter than forked lightning / they do not resist

their eye sockets beam amber to illuminate our way down the deep roads / I ask them another word for holy light and they say light with strings attached

after the uncrushable pigeon has been disposed of in a lava pit / I promise to take the ultimate war machine to a truly birdless place / eventually our roving warden band traverses many lands / to the shifting dunes where nothing warm-blooded can live

our caravan makes camp at the edge of the desert / only my golem keeps pacing forward with me / then carries my body

until I make my parched command / for them to lay down with me in the dirt / roll on top of me

they tell me I don't tremble like most animals

Notes

Winter Swimmers
'Tetrachromacy' first appeared in *Deluge*
'Spirit Animals' and 'Cosmic Rays' first appeared in *Zoomoozophone Review*
'House' first appeared in *Alien Mouth* and was reprinted in *Food Court*
'Winter Swimmers' (p. 8) first appeared in *Landfall*
'Redwing' first appeared in *Entropy Mag*
'Bigfaced Moons' first appeared in *Inferior Planets*
'The Car and the Man Inside' first appeared in *Minarets*
'Watch Your Mouth' first appeared in *Bound: An Ode to Falling in Love*
    (Compound Press, 2014) and was reprinted in *Oscen*
'The Year I Let My Heart Go Asunder' and 'Anne Brontë' first appeared
    in *Sweet Mammalian*
'Winter Swimmers' (p. 22) first appeared in *Oscen*
'Roller Coaster Hands' first appeared in *Illuminati Girl Gang*
'Winter Swimmers' (p. 27) first appeared in *The Spinoff*'s 'The Friday Poem'
'Hostage' first appeared in *Metazen*
'Earthquake Preparedness' first appeared in *PANK*

does a potato have a heart?
'we are working on standing still', 'complaint', 'notes on the girls with
    the red cardigans', 'does a potato have a heart?' and 'grace wakes late'
    first appeared in *Signals*
'unhatched egg/two girls at easter' first appeared in *The Spinoff*
'rocky shore' first appeared in *NZPS Anthology 2015*
'red brick, stamford street', 'I only took one photo of switzerland', 'january
    at the bloemenmarkt' and 'if you cannot draw good pictures' first
    appeared in *Starling*
'all the friendship bracelet makers have retreated' and 'do not blame
    me for loving the 2003 film love, actually' first appeared in *The
    Three Lamps*
'to keep all the bees out', 'apricot' and 'schön' first appeared in *Mimicry*

Softcore coldsores
'Primal scream practice', 'Gremlin in sundress', 'Meanwhile', 'Death by nectar',
    and 'Any machine can be a smoke machine if you use it wrong enough'
    first appeared in *Starling*
'Dairy queen' first appeared in *Scum Magazine*
'The flexitarian' first appeared in *Sport*
'The cave draws you in like a breath' first appeared in *Sweet Mammalian*

'Cold speculum', 'Add penetrant to preferred broadleaf herbicide & devastate the wildflowers' and 'If I could breed your cultivar I'd have you in my garden' first appeared in *Landfall*

'Would I recognise the garden if I saw it' and 'The land without teeth' first appeared in *Mayhem*

'Tropical snow' first appeared in *Turbine*

'Grooming' first appeared in the *Death & Desire* exhibition of hair at the Alexander Turnbull Library

'Crush', 'Barbecue mirage' and 'Biologist abandoned' first appeared in *Mimicry*

'Technicolour dreamcake': After Adrian Cox's oil painting *Border Creatures with Secret Life*' (2018).

'Biologist abandoned', 'Overladen trellis', and 'Shield your eyes for the bright of it': After Alex Garland's film adaptation (2018) of Jeff Vandermeer's novel *Annihilation* (2014).

'Death by nectar': After Marianne North's oil painting *A New Pitcher Plant from the Limestone Mountains of Sarawak, Borneo* (1876).

Carolyn DeCarlo lives in Aro Valley in Wellington, New Zealand, with her partner and cats. She has a BA from Georgetown University and an MFA from the University of Maryland, College Park. She is the author of four chapbooks, most recently *Green Place* (Enjoy Journal, 2015) and *Bound: An Ode to Falling in Love* (Compound Press, 2014), which she co-wrote with Jackson Nieuwland and which won Best Literary Zine at the 2015 Auckland Zinefest. She is a founding member of the Wellington-based reading collective *Food Court*. Her passions include film, art, tattoos and plants.

Sophie van Waardenberg was born in London and grew up in Auckland. She has a BA in English and history from the University of Auckland, and will soon be studying towards her MFA at Syracuse University. Her work has been published in *Starling*, *Mimicry*, *Best New Zealand Poems* and *The Spinoff*. She spends a lot of time browsing socks on the internet.

Rebecca Hawkes grew up on a high-country farm near Methven and now works, writes and paints in Wellington city. She holds an honours degree in media studies and an MA in creative non-fiction from the International Institute of Modern Letters at Victoria University of Wellington. Her poetry has been published in *Sport*, *Landfall*, *Starling*, *Mayhem*, *Sweet Mammalian* and elsewhere. She can usually be found writing, painting or painstakingly catching insects to feed her pitcher plant.

First published 2019
Auckland University Press
University of Auckland
Private Bag 92019
Auckland 1142
New Zealand
www.press.auckland.ac.nz

© Carolyn DeCarlo, Sophie van Waardenberg, Rebecca Hawkes, 2019

ISBN 9 781 86940 903 6

Published with the assistance of Creative New Zealand

A catalogue record for this book is available from the National Library of New Zealand

This book is copyright. Apart from fair dealing for the purpose of private study, research, criticism or review, as permitted under the Copyright Act, no part may be reproduced by any process without prior permission of the publisher. The moral rights of the authors have been asserted.

Design by Greg Simpson

Printed in Singapore by Markono Print Media Pte Ltd

AUP new poets 5

Carolyn DeCarlo
Sophie van Waardenberg
Rebecca Hawkes

Edited and with a foreword
by Anna Jackson

AUCKLAND
UNIVERSITY
PRESS